WHAT ARE YOU GOING TO dream ABOUT?

BY HAIM HALAWANI

What Are You Going to Dream About?
Copyright © 2019 by Haim Halawani

All rights reserved. No part of this publication may be reproduced, distributed, or transmitted in any form or by any means, including photocopying, recording, or other electronic or mechanical methods, without the prior written permission of the author, except in the case of brief quotations embodied in critical reviews and certain other non-commercial uses permitted by copyright law.

tellwell

Tellwell Talent
www.tellwell.ca

ISBN
978-0-2288-0701-8 (Paperback)

Dedicated to
Danielle Miah and Noa

This story is real.
This story is true.
This story is about,
a child like you.

Every night when it's time for bed, thoughts of the day go running through your head.

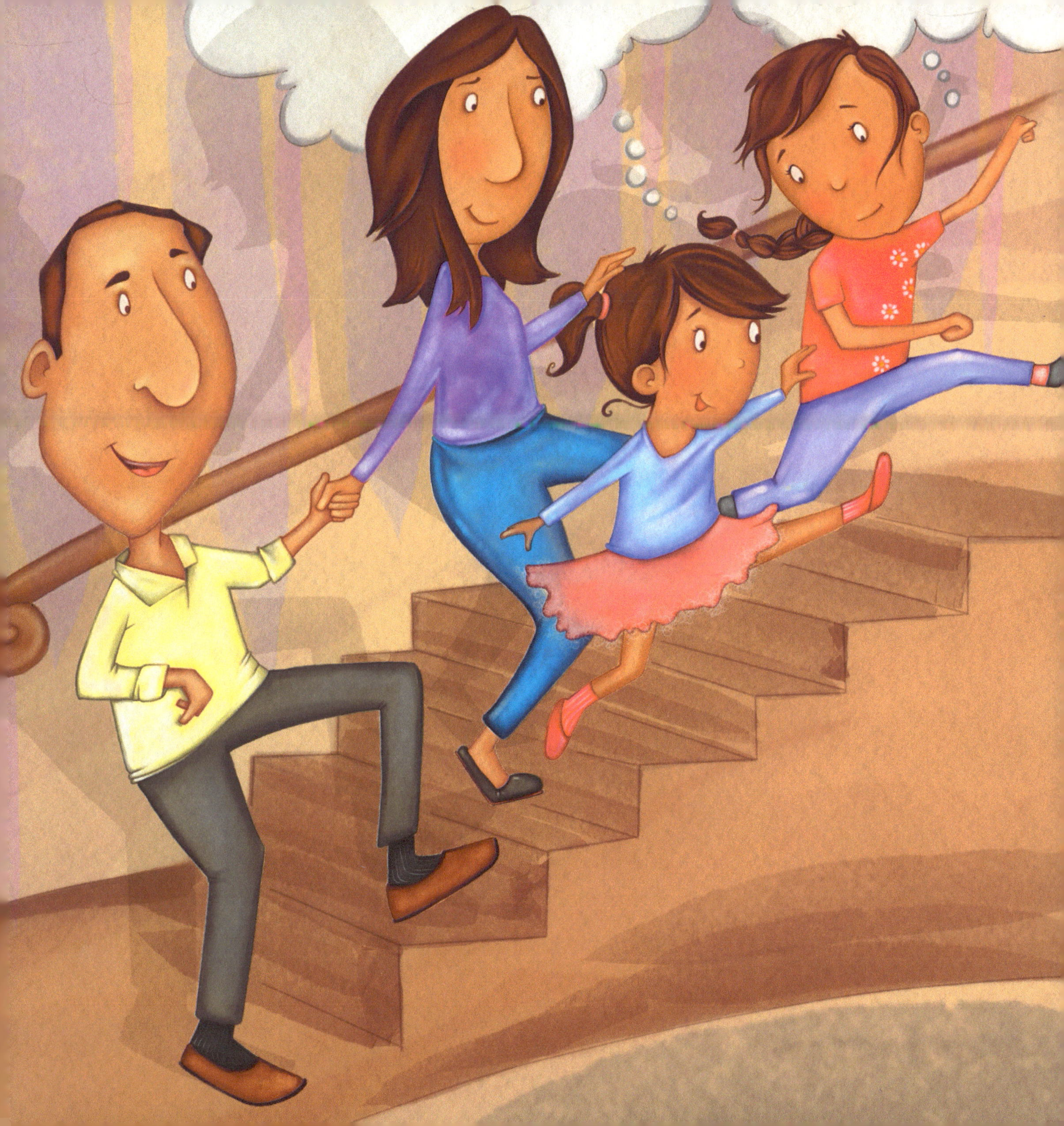

When it's time to put your head down for the night, you scream and cry and fight, fight, fight!

You toss and turn, turn and toss. You are only a child, but think you're the boss.

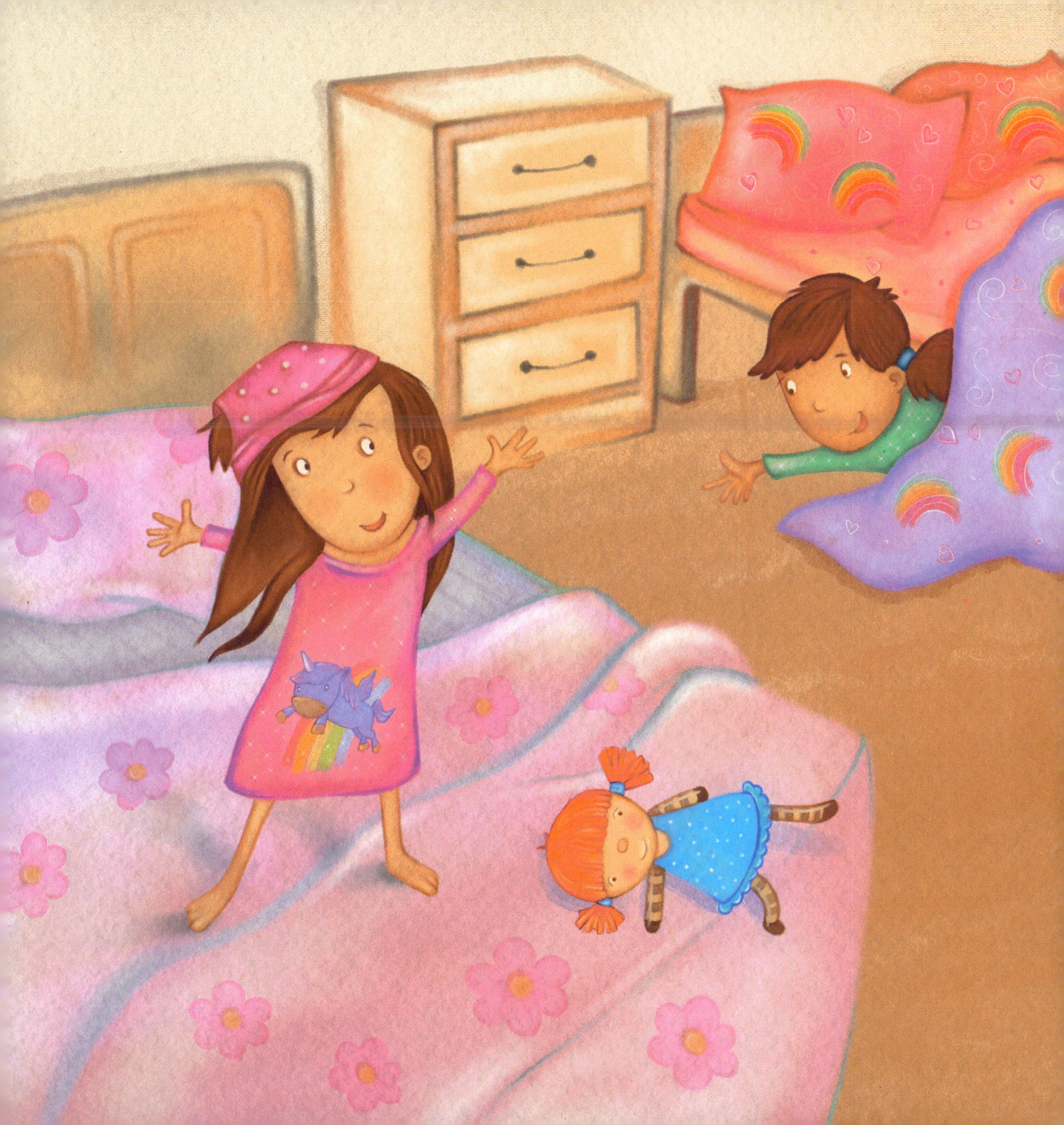

For every night when it's time for sleep, you give Mom and Dad a hard time, instead of going to bed without a peep.

When it's time to put your head down for the night, you toss and turn and fight, fight, fight!

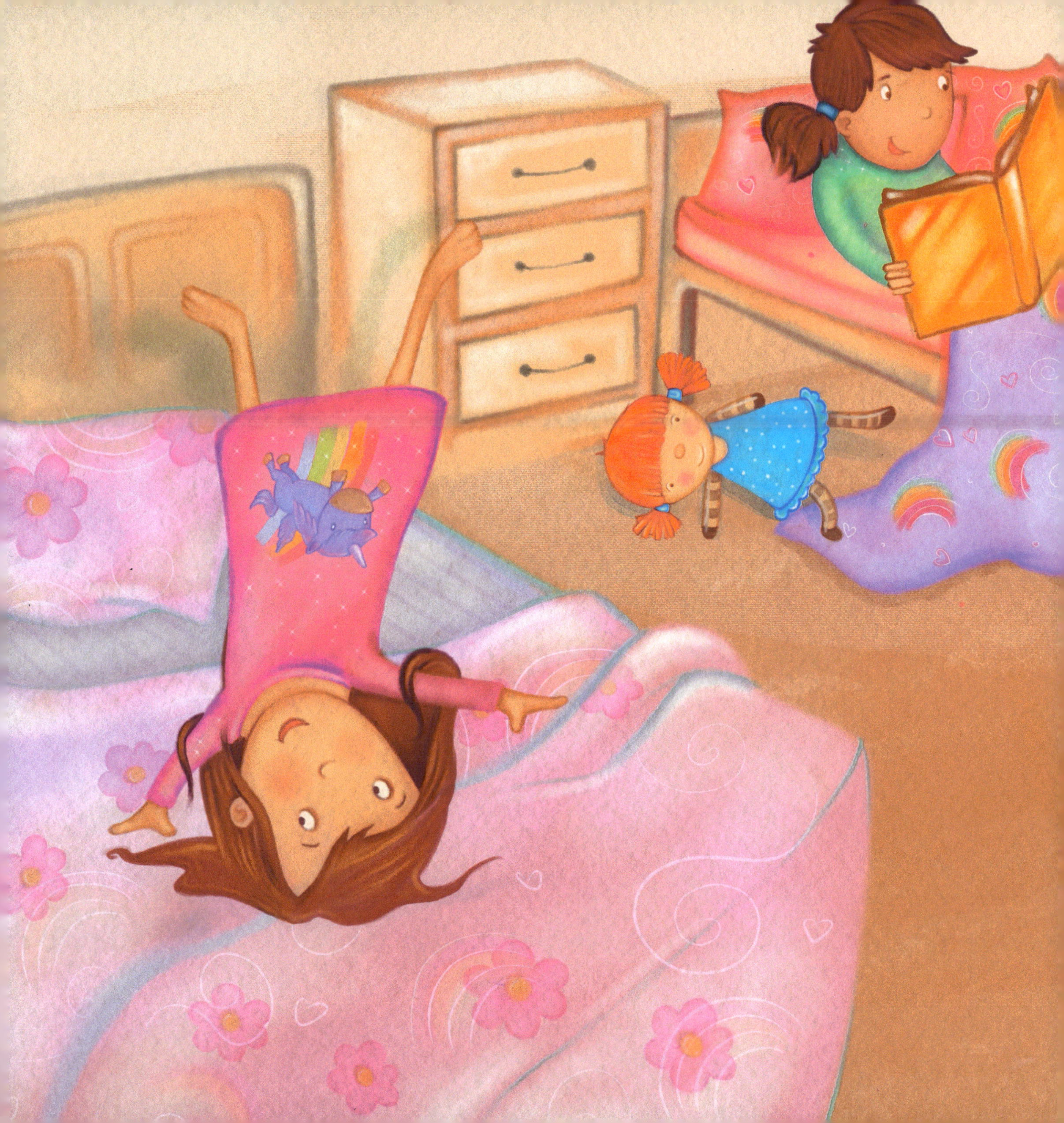

Weekday mornings, a story of two tales, you ask for the beach and to play with sand pails.

Mom and Dad say, "During the week you learn at school. The weekends are the times we do things that are cool."

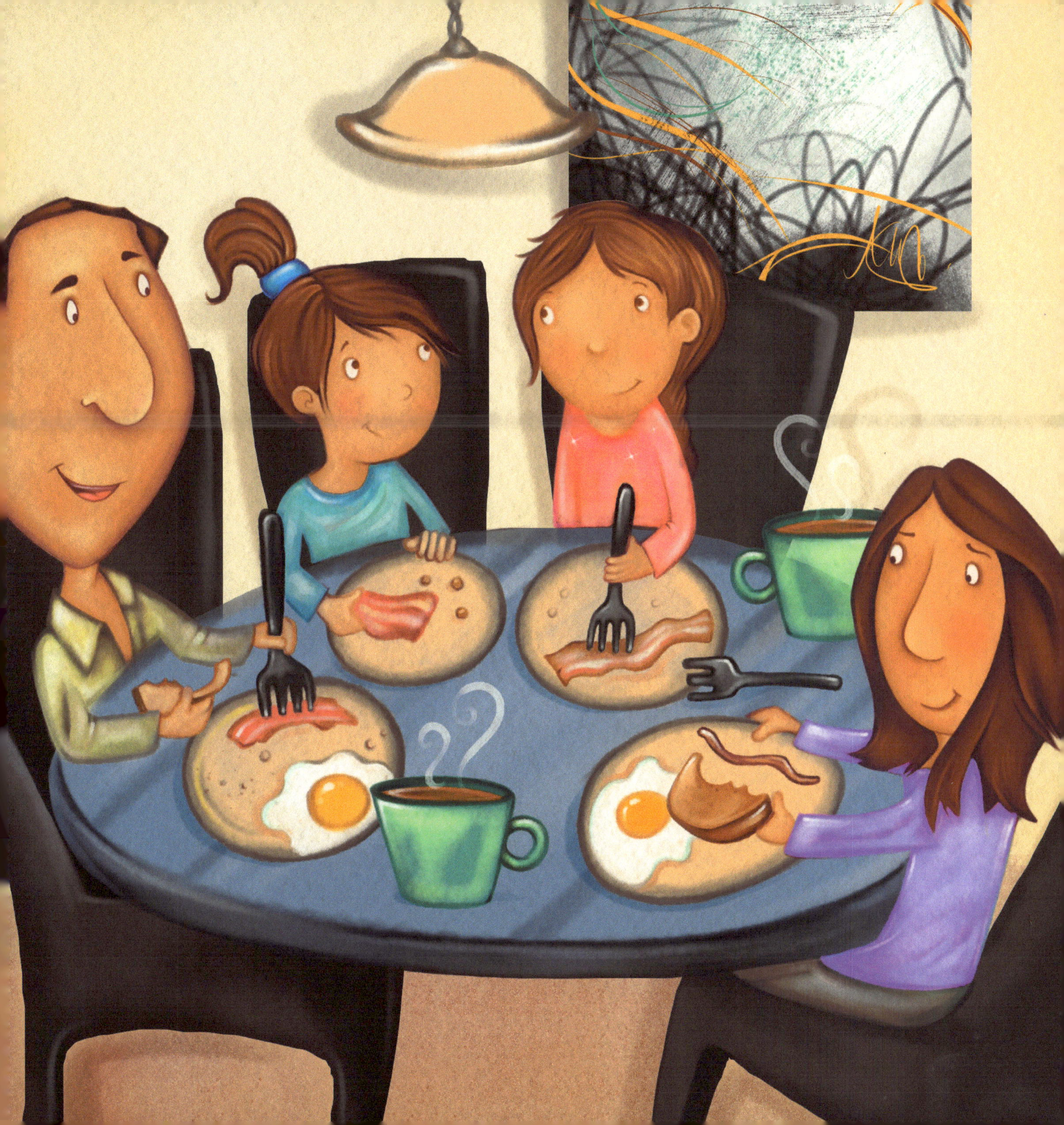

During the week, we spend time reading, writing and doing math. Home from school, relax, have dinner and take a bath.

But after all that is done with love in Mom and Dad's hearts. Bedtime comes around, and again the fun starts.

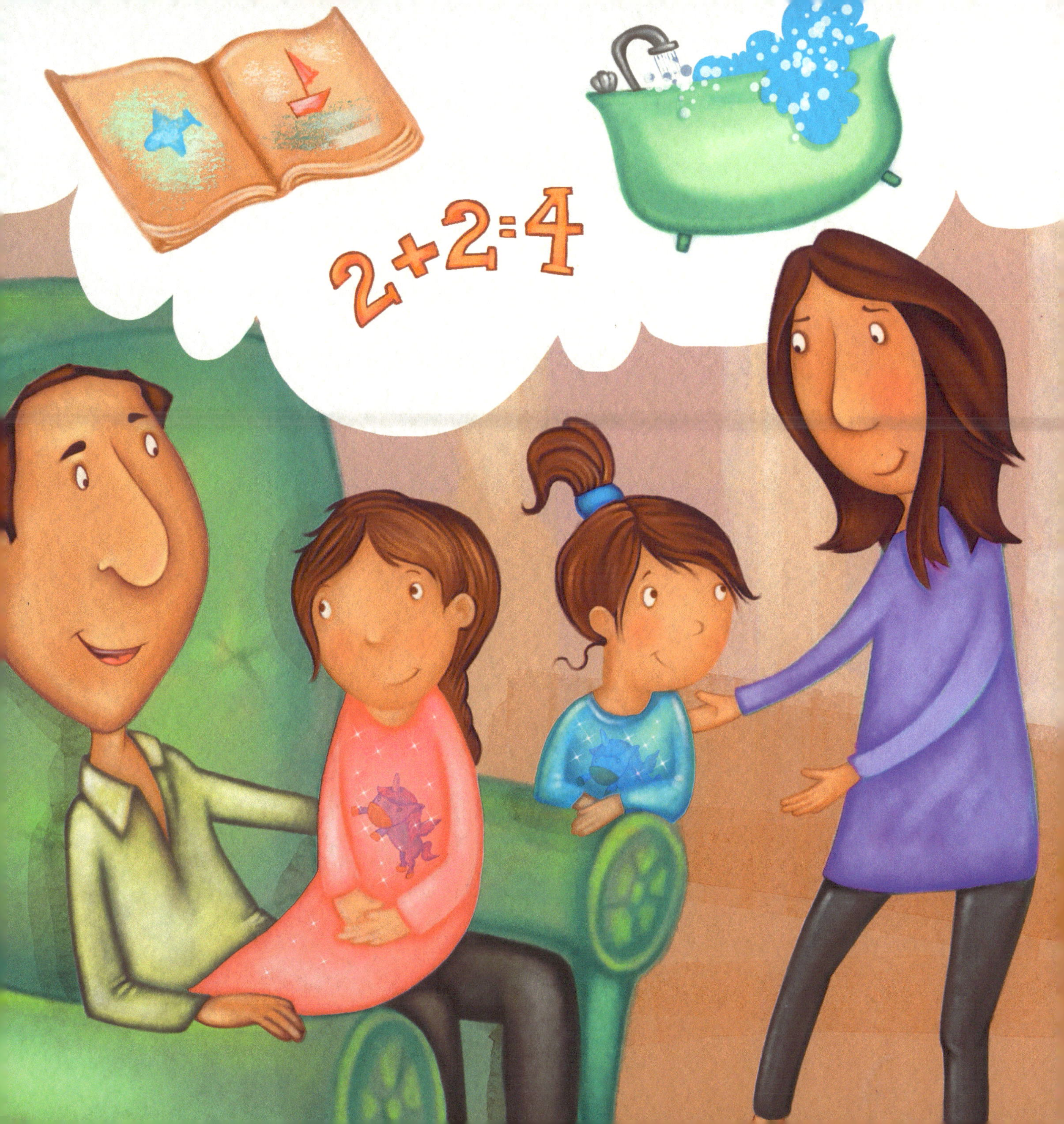
2+2=4

When it's time to put your head down for the night, you scream and cry and fight, fight, fight!

So, the next day, an idea pops into Mom and Dad's heads. Let's ask them a question right before bed. Let's ask them this question before they start to scream and shout.

"Tell me, my love, 'What are you going to dream about?'"

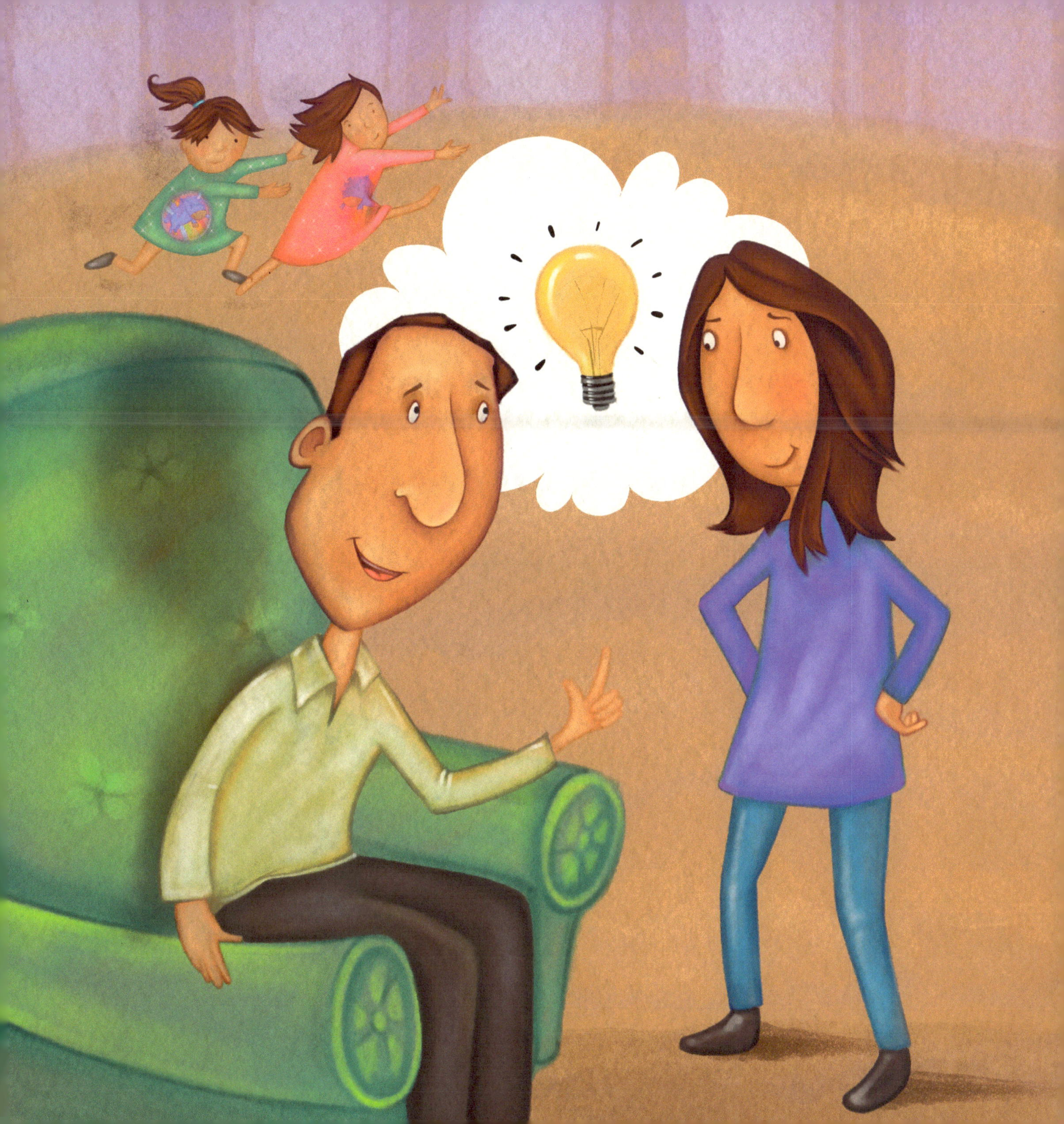

Mom and Dad looked at each other and hoped it would work, bed without crying...that would be a perk.

So, that night in the house, when it came time for bed, a new bedtime routine was formed instead. After learning, eating, reading and math, and right after a taking a nice long hot bath.

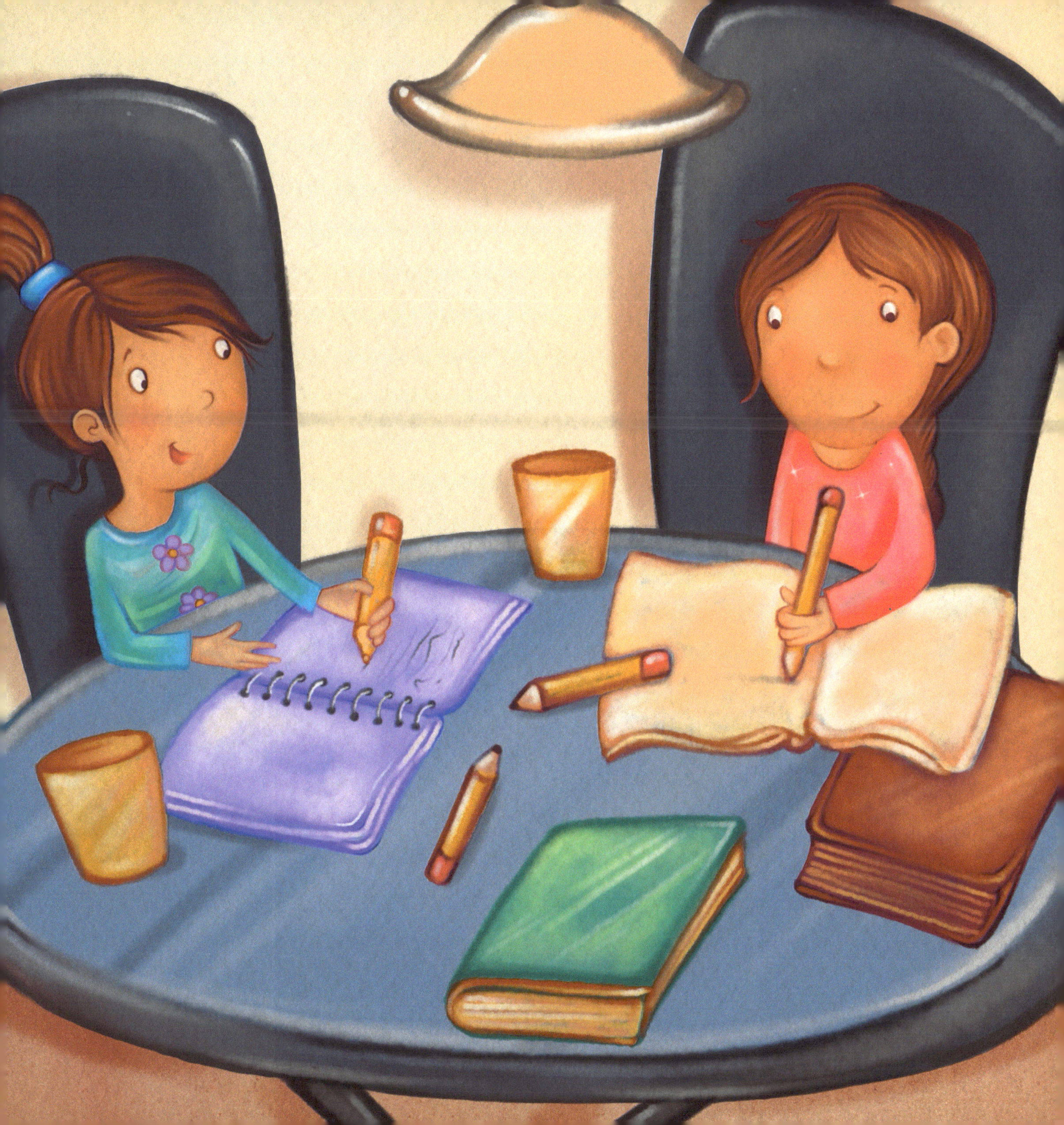

When the children, lying in bed, get ready to shout, instead, Mom and Dad asked this question: "Tell me, my love, what are you going to dream about?

The children's eyes lit up with answers so pure, could it be Mom and Dad have found a cure?

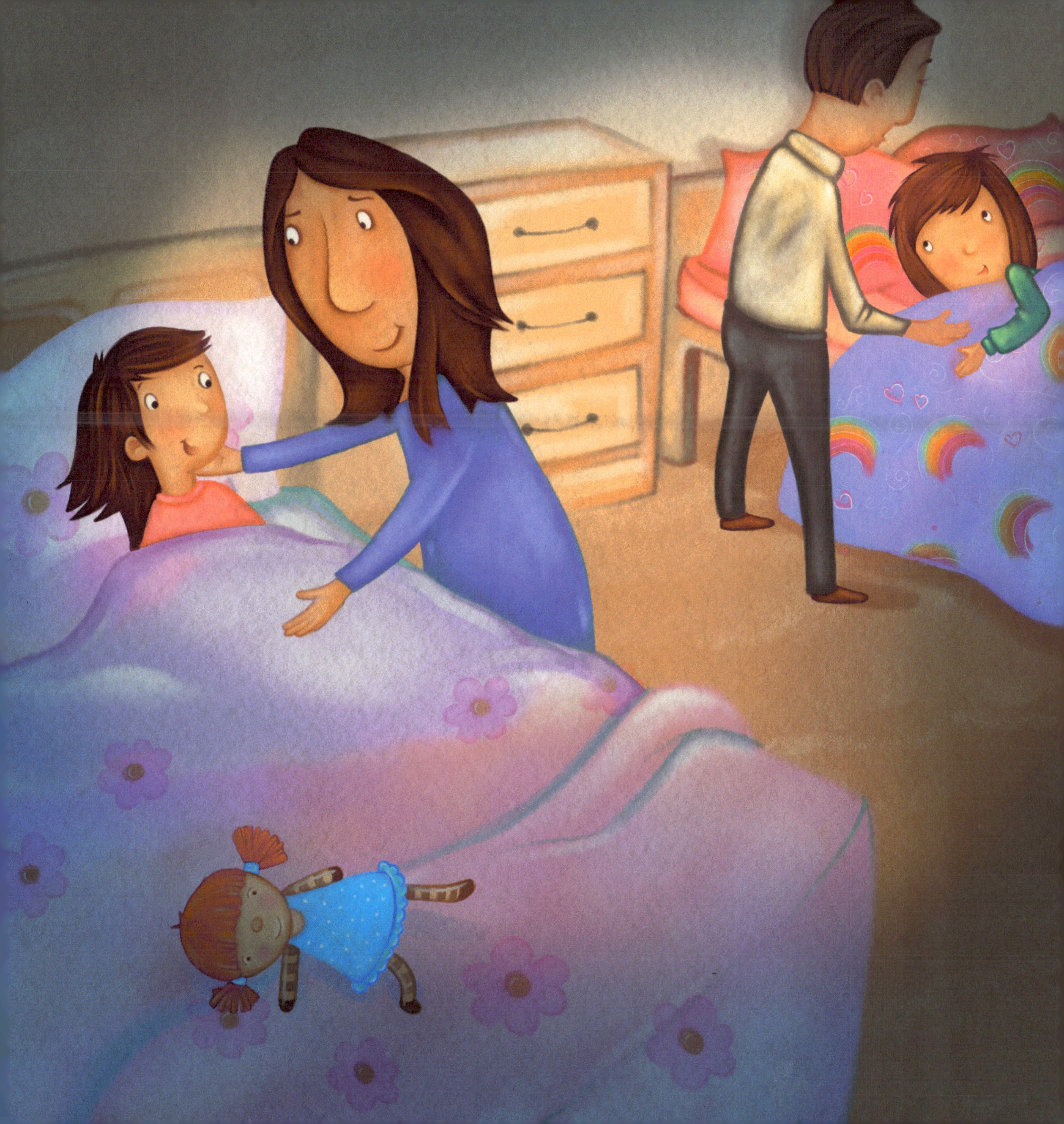

Miah the eldest couldn't wait to answer. We thought it would be to grow up a dancer. But what she said surprised Mom and Dad, and they were very impressed with the answer she had.

"I want to go to the beach and play in the sand or play games and swim at Canada's Wonderland. Put my bathing suit on and go to the splash pad. I think that's the greatest dream ideas I ever had."

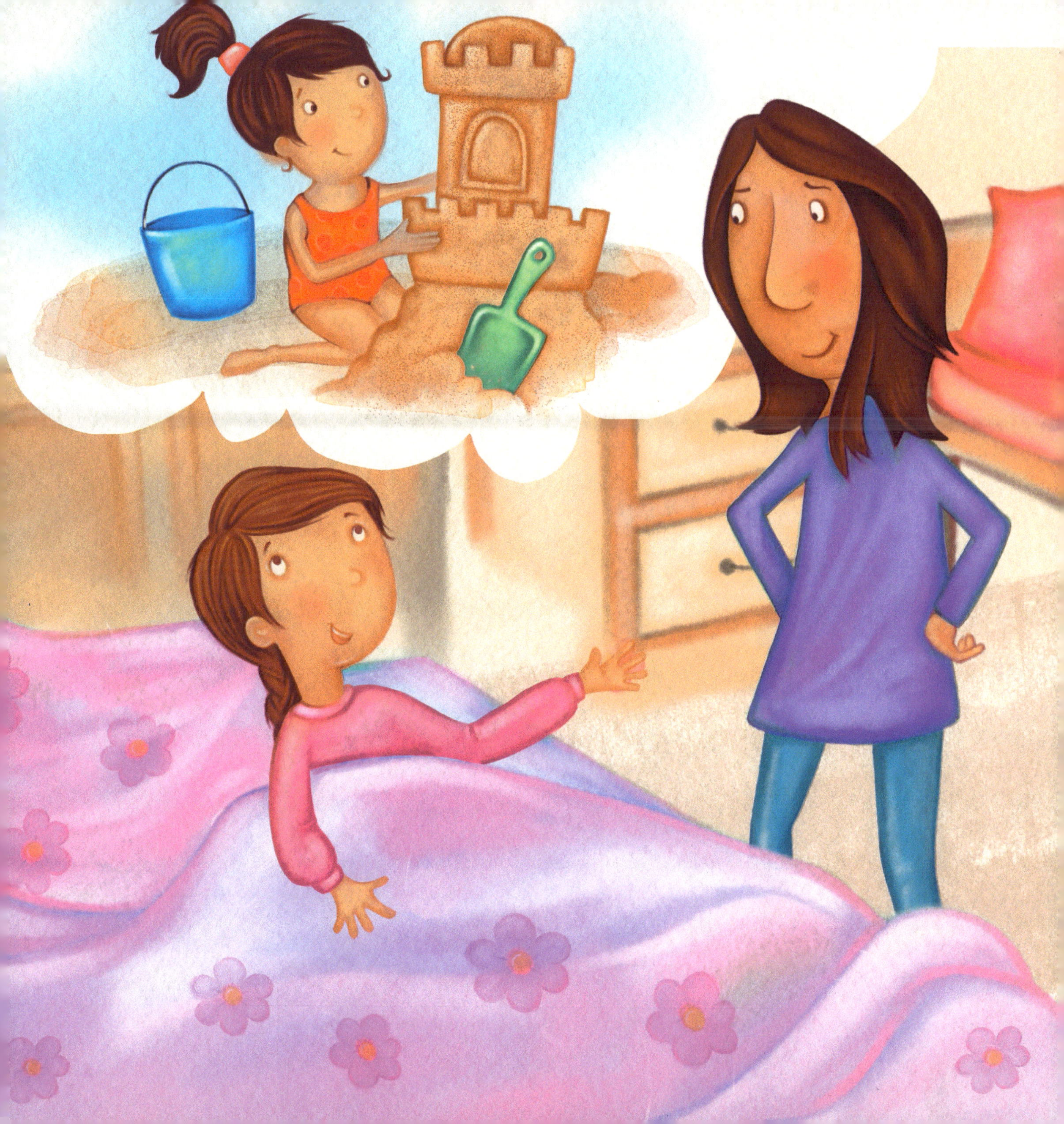

Noa the younger of the two sisters was lying in bed. The thought of dreams she will dream fluttered though her head.

"Mommy, Mommy, Daddy, Daddy, ask me, ask me, my answer will be amazing, you will see!" Then moving over to her sister who was waiting, the answer Mom and Dad were anticipating.

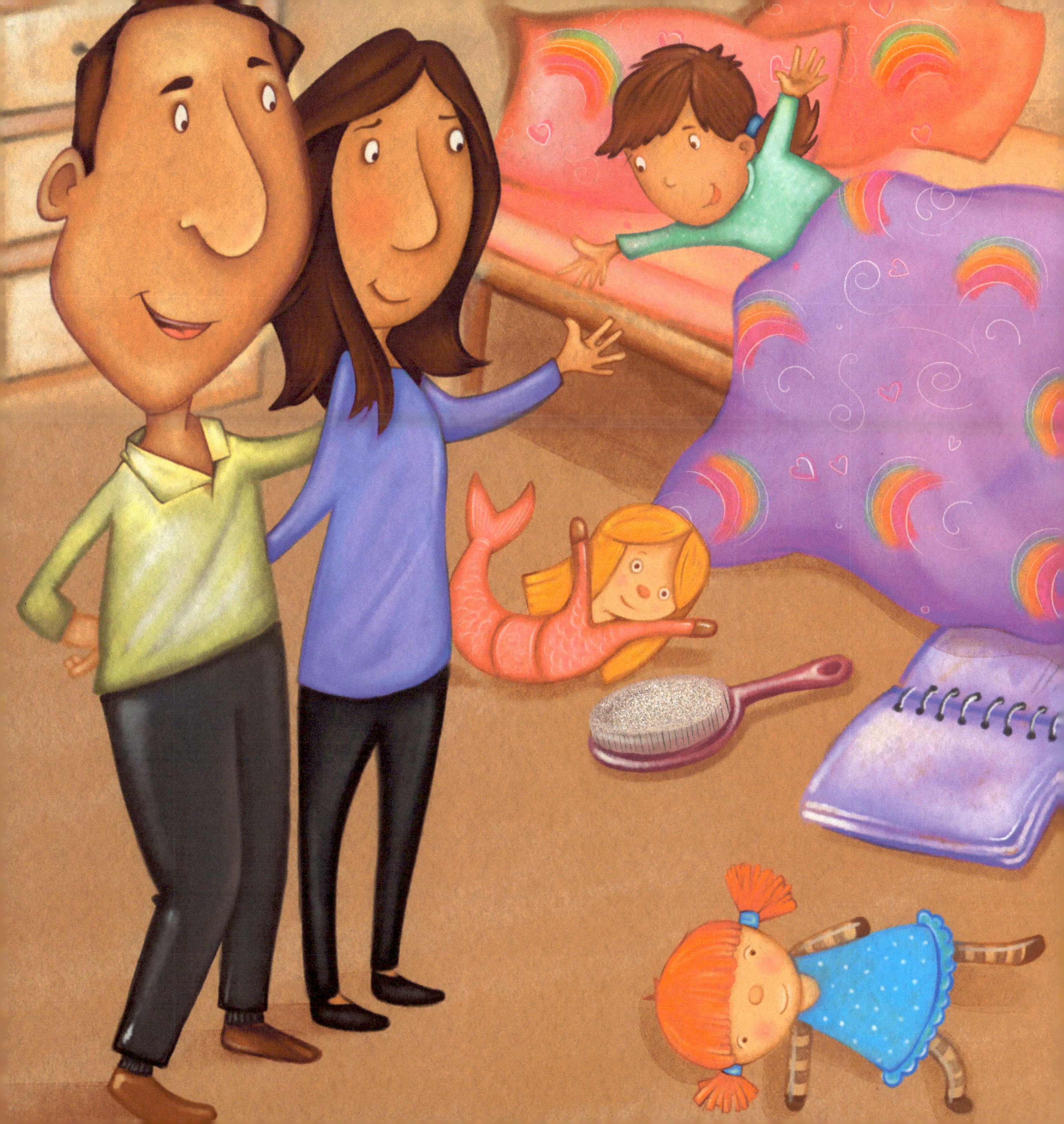

So, without any questions or any thought, they ask little Noa, "What are you going to dream about?"

Her answer differed a little from her big sister's. She started spinning and spinning waiting to answer like a twister.

"I'm going to dream about flowers, unicorns playing, and candy, a box for my toys."

Now that would be handy.

"I'm going to dream about Charlie our dog, my sister, and you." An answer Mom and Dad thought was so pure and true.

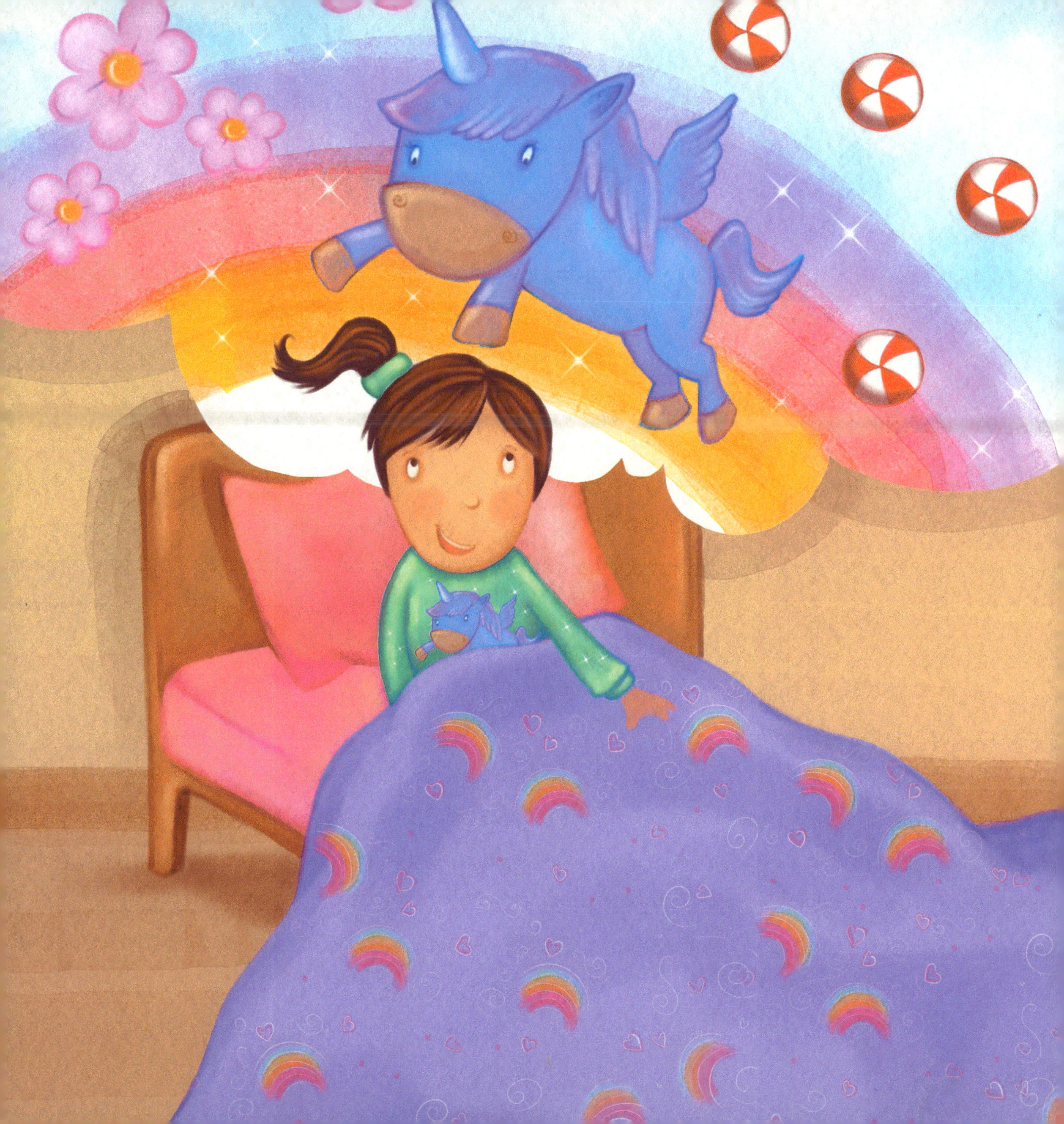

An unusual thing happened that night, a different approach left the kids without a fight. They went to bed happy and smiling and cozy in their sheets, happiness flowing from their heads down to their feet.

As the weeks went on, Mom and Dad questioned them nightly, and their answers changed ever so slightly.

From candies and unicorns to celebrating birthdays, dreams of growing up and going on holidays.

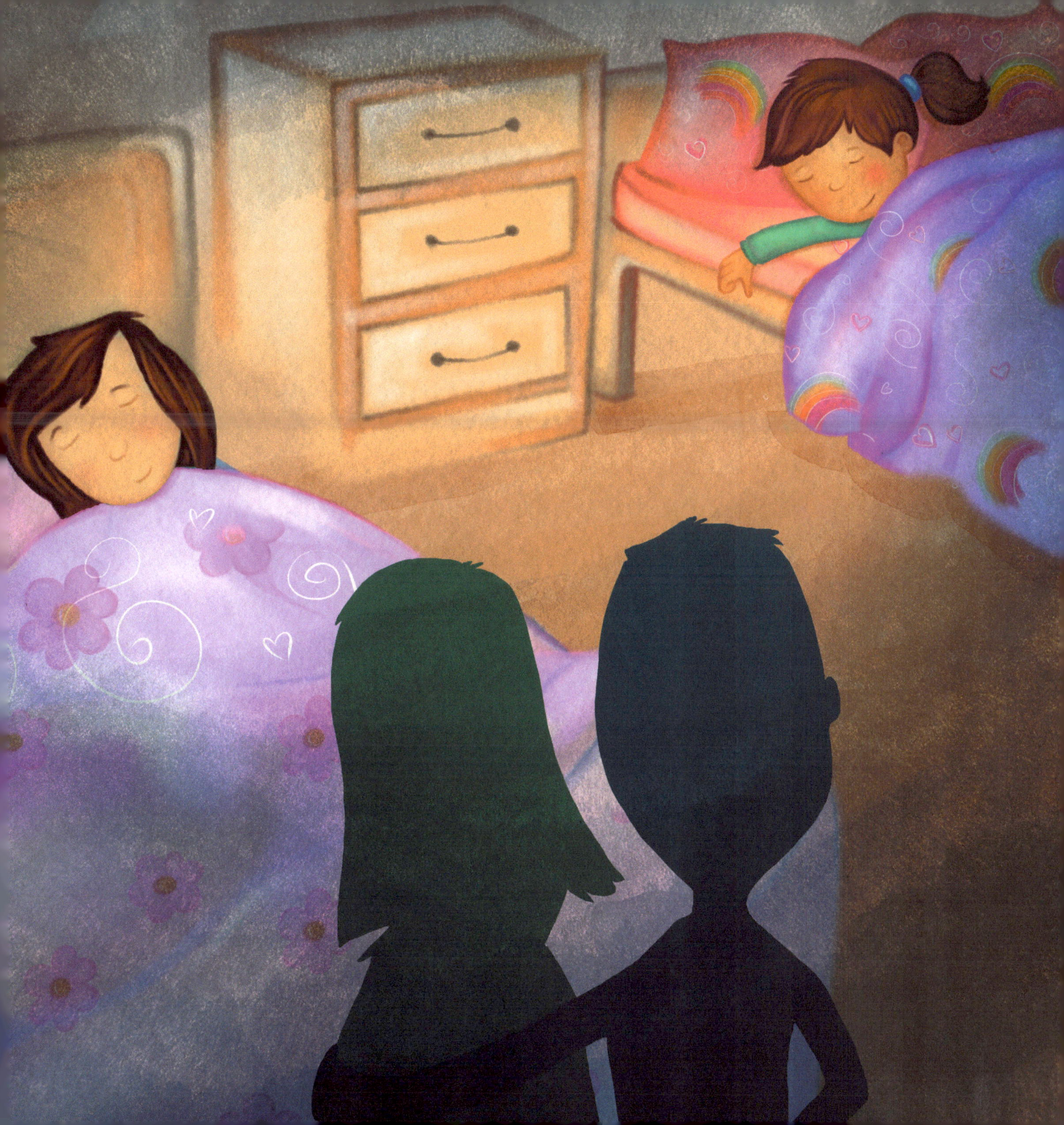

Mom and dad were so happy that their plan was working. Much better than the days of crying and smirking.

So, remember that no matter where on earth you are from, close your eyes, dream your dreams, and morning will come! So when it comes time for sleep and you have any doubt, ask them softly and nightly, "What are you going to dream about?"

CPSIA information can be obtained
at www.ICGtesting.com
Printed in the USA
LVHW072158040419
613044LV00002B/2/P